Moving fast and going nowhere!

Organizational Change and Employee Retention

Strange Bedfellows

Preface

Understanding organizational change and employee retention are vital for corporate leaders and small business owners. As we move further into the world of technology, we must not lose sight of the human aspects of business. No matter how technologically advance your business becomes, your stakeholders, and client base are still human. Humans' still desire personal attention, service that makes them feel good, and bring value. Employees and customers can view organizational change as good if value is the priority. Many healthcare organizations are moving from volume to value to reduce costly turnover and hiring.

Introduction

Organizational change (OC), change agility, change management, and employee retention all stem from numerous external and internal sources. One thing is commonly known about all four topics, and that is there will always be reasons for them. In this article, Employee retention is the primary area of importance regarding the change in an organization. Related topics covered in this book are (a) analysis of the field, (b) the current dilemmas, (c) current theories, (d) sustainability, (e) the impact of employee retention in the business industry, and (f) the future direction of this field.

Change agility or organizational agility is popular topics among many HRM executives (Horney, 2014). One critical factor of change agility is the organizational change management capability. Change agility is an attribute of an organization; it is a state of being (Horney, 2014). According to Horney (2014), an agile change model provides effective tools and processes that enable leaders, HR partners, and organizations to anticipate and exploit change with speed and flexibility. The new trend (i.e., Change Agility) enhances the origins of change management.

Across literature regarding change agility, change management capability is identified as a critical enabler (Horney, 2014). Building an organizational change management capability not only enables change agility, but it also results in a more effective application of change management. Also, to a more effective application, a higher success rate is achieved on change initiatives (Horney, 2014). In the article, *"From Change Projects to Change Agility,"* the authors examined the role of the chief human resource officer (CHRO) in equipping the organization to meet the challenge of corporate change. The authors outlined the characteristics of the human resource (HR) department with change agility, such as anticipating opportunities and threats, as well as shrewdness in rapidly adapting HR processes.

According to Demailly (2014), HRM leaders are looking for new perspectives on how to help their companies deal with change while maintaining sustainability. The current business environment requires businesses to be agile. Business agility is the ability to change businesses and business processes beyond the normal level of flexibility while managing unpredictable external and internal changes with ease (Oosterhout, 2006). The authors analyze factors requiring agility and assess agility gaps that companies are facing in four industry sectors in the Netherlands.

A framework was constructed to measure the perceived gaps between the current level of business agility and the required levels of business agility. The questionnaire and in-depth interviews conducted revealed that today's businesses perceive to lack the agility required to quickly respond to changes, whose speed and requirements are difficult to predict (Oosterhout, 2006). The authors presented rankings of generic and sector-specific agility gaps. These show that although some generic change factors requiring agility exist, the change factors requiring agility that cause agility gaps differ across industry sectors.

Among the factors that enabled or hindered business agility, the existence of inflexible legacy systems was perceived to be an important disabler in achieving business agility. Some basic principles and directions were discussed to transform barriers into a key enabler for increased agility in organizations and business networks. The authors introduced a reflective and critical rhetorical framework capable of replacing traditional approaches to change management and its education. The authors' framework indicates that managing change as the *mindful mobilizing of maps, masks, and mirrors* provided a comprehensive integration of the profession, practice, and critical academic literature on change management.

The authors used a dramatic approach, combining dramaturgical and pragmatic approaches to organizations and change. The authors introduced the framework, the manner of its delivery, and the varying perceptions of its nature. The impact on some mature middle management MBA students who had attended the course was also made available. The documentation of student interpretations draws on the learning diaries completed by MBA students in two deliveries of the subject at a leading business school in Australia.

The point of contention is that the framework provides a working model of a reflective and critical approach to change management that resonates with mature managers, and concludes with recommendations for future research and development. Although the authors' research was for solving the problem of how can casinos owners manage organizational change programs, and internal and external customer relationship management (CRM) programs the research aligns. The solution entailed two stages of qualitative methods: convergent interviewing and case research about four departments of a casino in Australia.

After the data analysis of documents and interview data, 12 themes were identified and led to the development of a model of how organizational change management and CRM can be integrated to improve initiatives in organizations such as casinos. The model has seven core elements: Vision, key challenge, objective, measure, strategy, initiative, and outcome. Even though the study was for customer relationship management in a casino, the seven elements could be used in any business or industry.

Analytic generalization beyond the research setting was made. However, external validation should be performed in future research. Managers of any business could use the checklist of actions about this research's integrated model, to reduce the high failure rate of change initiatives. Bushe (2015) wrote about people who are successful at facilitating transformational change have merged interpretivist social science, and complexity natural science in their thinking and practice.

Bushe (2015) discussed how complexity science could help AI practitioners deepen their thinking and improve their transformational change practice. Even though innovation is not the main theme of the article, the author outlines the process as transformational. Transformational is the act, or an instance of transforming and innovation is something new, the act of innovating. Both can be consider related.

Deserti and Rizzo (2014) argued that the idea of designing radically new products could bring about unexpected changes in the culture of a business enterprise. The development of significantly innovative products was suggested and could create contradictions between the current corporate culture and the one needed to implement the innovation. The authors proposed a bottom-up perspective on organizational change while criticizing top-down change management approaches particularly in regards to design thinking.

The author writes how the senior leaders' behaviors in the change management process affect the resulting outcome. Topics include the surveys conducted by the author with the assistance of the American Society for Quality (ASQ) advisory team for statistical analyses and the active demonstration of support and stakeholder preparation as the senior management behaviors with the largest gap between successful and unsuccessful change initiatives. Going back a moment to agility and its effects on organizational change or change management, leaders must be able to anticipate and exploit change with speed and flexibility. Hang on I will get to how organizational change, change agility, and change management affects employee retention.

Deserti and Rizzo (2014) wrote in the context of organizational change and the effects on employee morale regarding paid sick leave. The researchers examined employers' responses to San Francisco, California's 2007 Paid Sick Leave Ordinance Methods. They used the 2009 Bay Area Employer Health Benefits Survey to describe sick leave policy changes and the policy's effects on firm operations. The results of the study indicated that of the companies offering paid sick leave in San Francisco grew from 73% in 2006 to 91% in 2009, with large firms (99%) more likely to offer sick leave than are small firms (86%) in 2009.

Most firms (57%) did not make any changes to their sick leave policy, although 17% made a major change to sick leave policy to comply with the law. Companies beginning to offer sick leave reported reductions in other benefits (39%), worse profitability (32%), and increases in prices (18%) however better employee morale (17%) and high support for the policy (71%). Many employers (58%) reported some difficulty understanding legal requirements, complying administratively, or reassigning work responsibilities. There was a substantial increase in paid sick leave coverage after the mandate.

Employers reported some difficulties in complying with the law but supported the policy overall. Furthermore, the subordinate staff reported they appreciated the change and felt the employer cared about them. The article contained how corporate social responsibility (CSR) is a recognized and common part of business activity. Some of the regularly cited motives behind

CSR are employee morale, recruitment, and retention, with employees acknowledged as a key organizational stakeholder.

Regardless of the significance of employees in relation to CSR, relatively few studies have examined their engagement with CSR and the impediments relevant to this engagement. The exploratory case study-based research addresses this paucity of attention, drawing on one to one interviews and observation in a large UK energy company. A diversity of engagement found, ranging from employees who exhibited detachment from the CSR activities within the company, to those fully engaged in the CSR activities, and to others who were content with their own personal, but not organizational, engagement with CSR.

Some organizational context impediments, including poor communication, a perceived weak and low visibility of CSR culture, and lack of strategic alignment of CSR to business and personal objectives served to explain this diversity of employee engagement. The social exchange theory helped explore the volition that individual employees have towards their engagement with CSR activities, and to consider the implications of an implicit social, rather than explicit economic, contract between an organization and its employees in their engagement with CSR. However, consider how employee morale can support CSR and employee retention. The author notes that the solution to employee morale and retention issues is the ability of the manager to understand what is in the hearts and minds of their employees. The right dialogue can motivate employees to stick around and not just be part of the change, but help drive it.

Employee disengagement is the single most important factor in declining productivity, which leads to higher absenteeism, higher costs of doing business, and all-around poor performance. Employee morale and retention often fall prey to major changes and challenges in any organization. According to the author, managers must be aware of the "engagement cliff." The engagement cliff is where the current work environment is fine. The managers during this period do not engage the employees.

If the manager desires to maintain this atmosphere, he or she must pay attention, greet, and engage the employee. Respect and dignity are what employees appreciate and want. The author wrote three simple steps for sustaining good employee morale and retention (1) Institute a mentoring program (2) give the employees something to be proud of and (3) Always be truthful.

The three steps will aid in reducing employee frustration and uncertainty due to the recent healthcare changes. Because this time is, a time transition (change) and even confusion employers must be sensitive to their employees. If employees are unaware of what is happening, they will inform themselves, rumors will fly, and morale will drop. The author did a good job writing about long-term morale building strategies for business managers. Particularly with the focus on the importance for the managers to provide, mentoring programs for their employees, the impacts of charitable projects of organizations on their employees, and communication with truthfulness to employees as another morale and retention sustaining strategy in business.

Keywords: organizational change, change agility, change management, organizational agility, employee retention, sustainability, textual analysis

Organizational Change -Background

The Seminole work regarding organizational change (OC) originated from George Litwin and others during the 1960's (Burke & Litwin, 1992). The researchers indicated that motivation, individual needs, and values of employees play a significant role in retention (Burke, 1992). Burke and Litwin (1992) provided a model for organizational change in two contexts. The first was exploring organizational functioning and the second, organizational change. The authors wrote regarding the associations between how employee performance is affected and how effective change occurs.

Gleick (1987) noted that organizational change is a kind of chaos (p.27). Chaos affects performance and can result from poor communication (Thompson, 2016). An important aspect of organizational change is knowing the key drivers. Culture and communication issues rank as top drivers of successful and lasting change in a company (Stacey, 2011; Buchanan, 1999; and Northouse, 2013).

Buchanan (1999) wrote that issues of culture change and the lack of managers effectively communicating with employees produced severe consequences (p. 22). Employee turnover is a severe consequence stemming from culture change and the lack of managers ability to communicate effectively with employees (Buchanan, 1999). According to Carter (2015), employee turnover can be devastating to a company's bottom-line and not just in real cost.

Organizational change (OC) is a vital part of a company's long-term success (Luscher, 2008). Under the topic of OC and it's' effects on employee retention, three change aspects come to mind, performing, belonging, and organizing (Luscher, 2008). Middle managers should execute organizational change while managing subordinates emotions (Luscher, 2008). According to researchers, change can spur debilitating anxiety and defensiveness. Managers must remember how change induces controversy and resistance, regardless of support (Anderson, 2015).

Organizational Change – Analysis of the Field

Organizational change is a continuous moving target. Most business leaders' intention is to navigate through the world of organizational change with their key stakeholders intact. To further study, the phenomena of OC in the context of advancing the idea that employee retention is paramount, credible, and reliable information is presented in this article. Currently, the literature reviewed regarding the field of organizational change is evolving and paradox (O'Connor, 1995).

According to O'Connor (1995), organizational change is a "system contradiction" in itself (p. 770). The author explains how control, stability, predictability, rational, and economic results are what management wants. However, change and the processes it entails run counter to management interest (O'Connor, 1995). A dilemma looming around OC is employee retention, and the field of organizational change is comprised of this important area. An analysis of organizational change and its' effects on employee retention is further outlined in this article.

Current Dilemmas

American businesses face the challenge of replacing 70 million experienced and talented workers over the coming decades as the Baby Boomer generation retires (Oladapo, 2014). This challenge comes at a time when the American workforce is experiencing historically high unemployment, global security threats, shifts in the ethnic composition of its workforce, and economic sluggishness (Oladapo, 2014). The current literature lacks sufficient studies regarding Emotional Intelligence (EI) and its relationship to job satisfaction.

Additional research regarding EI is necessary to gain an understanding of how it can support employee retention through organizational change and change management (Oladapo, 2014; Mrkvicka, 2014; Kahn, 2013). The qualitative study design of Kahn (2013) not only addresses crisis management. The author went further to include the disturbance of relational systems after an organizational change or crisis event. The findings of Kahn's study contain descriptions of behavior some employees displayed over a long span of time after a major change event (Khan, 2013). The threats to validity for Kahn's study are limited in the context of understanding how relational disturbances within an organization occur during the organizational change process.

Current Theories

Current theories suggest that organizational change literature continues to be responsive to the changing aspects of present-day workplace demands (Armenakis, 1999). A new theory is on the rise for examining the relationship between Emotional Intelligence (EI), a relatively new construct, and job satisfaction and the role its supports in employee retention (Glodstein, 2014). Glodstein (2014) indicated that turnover at a public accounting firm had created a staffing crisis. Although the author utilized the field of accounting, this study applies to any business industry in the United States.

Researchers are currently studying the impending crisis of how American businesses will need to replace 70 million experienced and talented workers in the coming years. All this is due to the Baby Boomer community retiring (Oladapo, 2014). The conversation in the research community is that the relationship between EI and job satisfaction affects retention rates during organizational change. Emotional intelligence encompasses both interpersonal skills and stress management (Glodstein, 2014).

These two factors can weigh heavily on retention during a time of organizational change or a crisis event (Thompson, 2016). Because according to researchers change can spur debilitating anxiety and defensiveness (Anderson, 2015). Moreover, the findings from the Goldstein study indicated that job satisfaction is related to retention, and a link exists between EI and job satisfaction in jobs that require higher levels of emotional functioning (Glodstein, 2014; Pfeffer, 2013).

Sustainability and Organizational Change

The current literature from Alexandra (2014) indicated that managers tend to put greater emphasis on searching for innovation rather than efficiency to ensure a continuous progression in the organization and or to maintain business sustainability. Sustainability in the business world is considered as incorporating social, economic, and environmental factors into a business decision. Sustainability ethics is not environmental ethics. Environmental ethics is concerned with the moral relationship between humans and nature (Pearce, 2008).

Sustainability ethics is concerned with the moral aspects of the threefold relationship of humans with other contemporaries, future generations, and nature. It simultaneously analyses the moral aspects of this threefold relationship (Pearce, 2008). Sustainability and organizational change are related and a paradox at the same time. A new framework is emerging based on the integrative view on corporate sustainability (Hahn, 2015).

This framework emphasizes the need for a simultaneous integration of economic, environmental, and social dimensions without, emphasizing one over any other (Hahn, 2015). The integrative view presumes that companies need to accept tensions in corporate sustainability and pursue different sustainability aspects simultaneously even if they seem to contradict each other (Hahn, 2015). The framework goes beyond the traditional triad of economic, environmental, and social dimensions and argues that tensions in corporate sustainability occur between different levels, in change processes and within a temporal and spatial setting.

The Hahn (2015) provides the vital groundwork for managing tensions in corporate sustainability based on paradox strategies. The author then applies the framework to identify and characterize four selected tensions and illustrates how key approaches from the literature on strategic contradictions, tensions, and paradoxes-i.e., acceptance and resolution strategies can be used to manage these tensions.

Hahn refines the emerging literature on the integrative view for the management of tensions in corporate sustainability. The framework also provides managers with a better understanding of tensions in corporate sustainability and enables them to embrace these tensions in their decision-making.

Industry Impact - Organizational change and employee retention has lasting impacts on any business. According to Cullen (2014), organizational change and the characteristics of change receivers influence their reactions to the change initiated in the workplace. Senior Management and Middle managers should step back and assess if they desire to continue on their current path or employ a new way of initiating change and begin to address the behavior that results from it. I strongly suggest leadership assume the latter position to remain competitive in this ever-changing economy. What may appear to be working now is not guaranteed to work in the future.

Future Direction - New trends in the field of organizational change management are: (a) the outside-in innovation, (b) social media as an innovation tool, (c) war games, (d) sustainability, corporate social responsibility and shared value, (e) brightsizing, (f) business analysis focused on design, and (g) better communication (Alexandra, 2014). I will only address a few in this article.

Outside-in-innovation is a game changer. Organizational leaders obtain unique solutions by viewing organizational problems in a new way. Here are a few strategies that will support the outside-in-innovation process: (a) think like your competitors.

What would put you out of business? Engage your stakeholders and collaborate on what are the threats to your business, then begin change initiatives, (b) Engage in different kinds of partnerships. A secure fire way to improve your business is to partner with other groups that add value to your organization, and (c) think beyond demographics. What are the unmet needs of your consumers? More importantly, how will you find out? Engage your client base, make a team out of them and ask them what are some of their unmet needs.

Better Communication – We are forever talking about this topic and still are not getting it right, why? I believe because some of us are incapable of building constructive relationships. Communication is the overriding action that can produce a successful outcome and build relationships of trust (Khan et al., 2013). Simply put, communication is a way to establish an understanding of people. Also, the researcher (i.e., Libenau, 2003) also indicated that effective communication is dependent on two areas (a) technology and (b) relationships.

Sustainability – Organizational change, job creation, innovation, and social change are drivers for sustainability (Taneja et al., 2016). New thinking and new choices are vital in a world of growing interdependence (Senge, 2010). Now more than ever removing limitations and minimizing consequences to sustain normal management attention is required.

The organizational leader's focus must be on seeing the larger systems in which businesses operate (Senge, 2010). After reading, some of the literature on sustainability and organizational change the apparent gap in the literature is linking the tensions of organizational change to management and organizational foresight. Despite the limits of predicting change taking place inside and outside organizations, anticipating crucial developments are possible. According to Oner (2014), businesses private and public need to use foresight as a way to shape and move toward desired futures for sustainable development in continuously changing and dynamic environments. If organizations intend to thrive in their change drive and take strategic actions by engaging with foresight projects, it would be wiser to create a foresight attitude among managers and decision makers in organizations while reducing tensions.

Conclusion

The effectiveness of HRM practices in tackling employee retention can be enhanced by improving the compatibility between an employee and organizational values. Some researchers test this hypothesis by using structural equation modeling on a sample of 258 employees in business process outsourcing (BPO) companies in the Philippines (Presbitero et al., 2016). The results of the study indicated that the relationship between employee and organization values positively and in some measure supports the effects of HRM practices on employee retention. On the other hand, employee–organization value conflicted in United States-owned BPOs. The findings also indicated a negative effect on employee retention because employees are less likely to leave when they share similar values as their organizations. HRM practices can be used strategically to improve the employee–organization value fit to improve retention. The implications of the findings for HR managers of BPOs in developing countries are promising.

Block (2016) offers tips on how to improve employee recruitment and retention in the U.S. healthcare sector in the middle of the regulatory changes being implemented in the industry. Also mentioned are the shift to the value-based health care delivery system from volume-based due to such developments as clinical transformation and improvements among accountable care organizations, as well as the need for continuous learning and skill development throughout a physician's professional career. Sheth (2016) explored how employers can get better talent retention, employee engagement, productivity, innovation, and great results by understanding the millennial mindset. More than money motivates Millennials. The need is to understand our employees' motivations and ambitions are paramount. Corporate leaders must become "vulnerable leaders" to achieve the results in business they desire. A vulnerable leader focuses more on the human and personal perspective of employee retention. Again, it is about aligning the employee with the values of the organization.

Barger's (2016) study findings indicated that women earned 49 percent of all science and engineering bachelor's degrees, 43 percent of science and engineering master's degrees and 40 percent of science and engineering doctoral degrees in 2014, reported by the National Student Clearinghouse. Women make up less than 25 percent of the STEM workforce and only 10.5 percent of employed engineers. Researchers have found that workplace culture and women's personal character traits (values) play major roles in retention. So what are the things that make a difference?

Acikgoz et al., (2016) examine the relationship between perceived employability and turnover intentions that is much more complicated than what common sense would suggest. Based on the reviewed literature, it was expected that job satisfaction, emotional commitment, and perceived job security would moderate this relationship. Using a sample of working individuals from different occupations and sectors, it was found that employees who perceived themselves as highly employable were more likely to have turnover intentions when their emotional commitment was low and perceived job security was high; and the relationship was negative for employees with shorter tenures. Understanding the conditions under which perceived employability is associated with turnover intentions may help organizations design human resource policies that allow them to retain an educated and competent workforce. I disagree with this premise and do not understand how simple the solution is with a limited number of employers getting right. Employees want to be valued, respected, and earn a fair wage. They want their leadership to be honest and truthful. How hard is that to comprehend?

Remember that old saying "a *little sugar goes a long way*"? Pay attention leaders of large and small corporations here lays great opportunities to dominate your market. Companies like Starbucks, Airbnb, LinkedIn, and Facebook are companies where people love to work. Employee retention, job satisfaction, organizational change, employee behavior, and sustainability are about more than money. It is also about the values, relationship, and effective communication. Things to remember are that communication consists of verbal and non-verbal actions, listening, and seeking help. Good communication is vital for healthy relationships and allows us to share our interest, values, objectives, and apprehensions. Organizational change and employee retention are worthy goals for which a company's leadership should strive.

References

Acikgoz, Y., Canan Sumer, H., & Sumer, N. (2016). Do employees leave just because they can? Examining the perceived employability- turnover intentions relationship. *Journal of Psychology, 150* (5), 666-683. doi:10.1080/0023980.2016.1160023

Alexandra, M., & Ion, M. (2014). New trends in management. *Annals of The University of Oradea, Economic Science Series, 23*(1), 1194-1199. Retrieved from http://econpapers.repec.org

Andersson, G. (2015). Resisting organizational change. *International Journal of Advanced Corporate Learning, 8*(1), 48-51. doi:10.3991/ijac.v8i1.4432

Armenakis, A. A., & Bedeian, A. G. (1999). Organizational change: A review of theory and research in the 1990s. *Journal of Management, 25*(3), 293-315 doi:10.1177/014920639902500303

Badham, R., Cançado, V. L., & Darief, T. (2015). An Introduction to the 5M Framework: Reframing Change Management Education. *BAR - Brazilian Administration Review, 12*(1), 22-38. doi:10.1590/1807-7692bar2015140033

Bager, T. S. (2016). Strategies for retaining female engineers. *IEEE Spectrum, 53* (7), 22. doi:10.1109/MPEC.2016.7498151

Block, D. J. (2016). Understanding recruitment and retention. *Physician Leadership Journal, 3* (4), 44-47.

Buchanan, D., Claydon, T., & Doyle, M. (1999). Organisation development and change—The legacy of the nineties. *Human Resource Management Journal, 9*(2), 20–37. Retrieved from http://www.tandfonline.com

Burke, W. W., & Litwin, G. H. (1992). A causal model of organizational performance and change. *Journal of Management, 18*(3), 523-545. Retrieved from http://www.sciencedirect.com/science

Carrison, D. (2014). The challenge of 2014: Sustaining morale. *Industrial Management, 56*(1), 6. Retrieved from http://www.journals.elsevier.com/industrial-marketing-management/

Carter, T. (2015). Hire right the first time. *Journal of Property Management, 80*(3), 26-29. Retrieved from http://www.emeraldgrouppublishing.com

Charlie Chi Cong, M., Perry, C., & Loh, E. (2014). Integrating Organizational Change Management and Customer Relationship Management in a Casino. *UNLV Gaming Research & Review Journal, 18*(2), 1-21. Retrieved from https://www.unlv.edu/hotel

Colla, C. H., Dow, W. H., Dube, A., & Lovell, V. (2014). Early effects of the San Francisco paid sick leave policy. *American Journal of Public Health, 104*, 2453-2460. doi:10.2105/AJPH.2013.301575

Cowart, L. (2014). Why employee morale matters--especially now. *Public Manager, 43*(1), 44-47. Retrieved from https://www.td.org/Publications/Magazines/The-Public-Manager

Cullen, K., Edwards, B., Casper, W., & Gue, K. (2014). Employees' adaptability and perceptions of change-related uncertainty: Implications for perceived organizational support, job satisfaction, and performance. *Journal of Business & Psychology, 29*, 269-280. doi:10.1007/s10869-013-9312-y

Demailly, C., & Brighton, D. (2014). HR, Be the Change You Wish to See!. *People & Strategy, 37*(1), 4. Retrieved from http://www.hrps.org

Deserti, A., & Rizzo, F. (2014). Design and the Cultures of Enterprises. *Design Issues, 30*(1), 36-56.

Gleick, J. (1987). *Chaos: Making a new science. New York, New York: Viking Publishing*

Glodstein, D. (2014). Recruitment and retention: Could emotional intelligence be the answer. *Journal of New Business Ideas & Trends, 12*(2), 14-21. Retrieved from http://www.worldcat.org/title/journal-of-new-business-ideas-trends

Hahn, T., Pinkse, J., Preuss, L., & Figge, F. (2015). Tensions in corporate sustainability: Towards an integrative framework. *Journal of Business Ethics, 127*(2), 297-316. doi:10.1007/s10551-014-2047-5

Horney, N., Eckenrod, M., McKinney, G., & Prescott, R. (2014). From Change Projects to Change Agility. *People & Strategy, 37*(1), 40-45. Retrieved from http://www.hrps.org

Lushcher, L. S., & Lewis, M. W. (2008). Organizational change and managerial sensemaking: Working through paradox. *Academy Of Management Journal, 51*(2), 221-240. doi:10.5465/AMJ.2008.31767217

Maurer, R. (2014). The Influence of Senior Leaders in Successful Change. *Journal for Quality & Participation, 37*(2), 4-9.

Northouse, P. G. (2013). *Leadership: Theory and practice (6th ed.).* Thousand Oaks, CA: SAGE.

O'Connor, E. S. (1995). Paradoxes of participation: Textual analysis and organizational change. *Organization Studies, 16*, 769-803. doi:10.1177/017084069501600502

Oladapo, V. (2014). The impact of talent management on retention. *Journal of Business Studies Quarterly, 5*(3), 19-36. Retrieved from http://jbsq.org

Oosterhout, M., Waarts, E., & Hillegersberg, J. (2006). Change factors requiring agility and implications for IT. *European Journal of Information Systems, 15*, 132–145. doi:10.1057/palgrave.ejis.3000601

Pearce, O. (2008). Holistic assessment of sustainability and its application at Halcrow. *Journal of Corporate Citizenship*, 30, 37–65. Retrieved from http://www.greenleaf-publishing.com

Pfeffer, J. (2013). You're still the same: Why theories of power hold over the time across contexts. *Academy of Management perspectives*, *27*(4), 269-280. doi:10.5465/amp.2013.0040

Presbitero, A., Roxas, B., & Chadee, D. (2016). Looking beyond HRM practices in enhancing employee retention in BPO's: Focus on employee-organisation value fit. *International Journal of Human Resources Management*, *27* (6), 635-652. doi:10.1080/09585192.2015.1035306

Ramos, C. Q., & Rees, C. J. (2008). The current state of organization development: Organizational perspectives from Western Europe. *Organization Development Journal*, *26*(4), 67-80. Retrieved from http://www.scimagojr.com

Sheth, M. (2016). How to achieve a win/win for both employees and corporates. *Strategic HR Review*, *15* (2), 70-75. doi:10.1108?SHR-02-2016-0011

Slack, R., Corlett, S., & Morris, R. (2015). Exploring employee engagement with (corporate) social responsibility: A social exchange perspective on organisational participation. *Journal of Business Ethics*, *127*, 537-548. doi:10.1007/s10551-014-2057-3

Stacey, R. (2011). *Strategic management and organizational dynamics: The challenge of complexity*. (6th ed.) Harlow, England: Pearson Education Limited.